Eileen Isagon Skyers

I0436379

Vanishing Acts

LINK
EDITIONS

Eileen Isagon Skyers
Vanishing Acts

Publisher: LINK Editions, Brescia 2015
www.linkartcenter.eu

This work is licensed under the Creative Commons
Attribution-NonCommercial-ShareAlike 3.0 Unported License.
To view a copy of this license, visit http://creativecommons.org/licenses/by-nc-sa/3.0/
or send a letter to Creative Commons, 171 Second Street,
Suite 300, San Francisco, California, 94105, USA.

Printed and distributed by: Lulu.com
www.lulu.com

ISBN 978-1-326-44735-9

Eileen Isagon Skyers has worked in contemporary art and non-profit arts organizations including the USF Contemporary Art Museum (Tampa, FL), The Wassaic Project (Brooklyn, NY), and the Portland Institute for Contemporary Art (Portland, OR). Her moving-image work has been exhibited nationally and internationally at Littman Gallery (Portland, OR), Spielberg Theatre (LA), the International Streaming Festival for Audiovisual Art (The Hague, NL) and Superchief Gallery (NYC) among others. She holds a BA in Philosophy and a BA in Studio Art from the University of South Florida, Tampa, FL and an MA in Critical Theory and Creative Research at Pacific Northwest College of Art, Portland, OR.

http://eiskyers.com

In this piece of writing, I look at the role of network-based art practices as an aesthetic critique of our engagement with interface technologies that are increasingly seamless and, largely, undetectable. It is worth noting that this text was originally conceived in partial fulfillment of the MA in Critical Theory and Creative Research at Pacific Northwest College of Art, under the title On Internet Art: A Critique of the Imperceptible Interface. *When my line of inquiry began, it was largely focused on Internet art and this concept of seamlessness, or transparency, that seems to drive current information culture. I've felt strongly that there's a direct correlation between the imperceptible interface and the distracted nature of human cognition. There are certain urgencies assailing our nervous systems now that, I'm convinced, were simply never there before. And despite our endless customization of web content, we're unable to observe the computational processes that make the information manifest. I became preoccupied with net art, and its capacity to reveal something quite crucial about the changing nature of subjectivity in relation to technology's gradual "vanishing act." Net art often employs retromediation and anachronism to call into question some of the actions inherent to networked space. These practices subvert the ruling tendencies and assumptions of screen-based operation, namely, transparency and interactivity.*

The ideas laid out herein simply could not have come to their full fruition without the guidance of Anne-Marie Oliver, Barry Sanders, Joan Handwerg, Marie-Pierre Hasne, and Robert Lawrence. Together, they have motivated the exactitude and rigor of my personal understanding of the meaning of, and necessity for, critique - and for that, I have to express my gratitude.

This publication is dedicated to my mom, who has provided unquestioning acceptance and support.

Contents

Introduction

Fig. 1. Jaakko Pallasvuo, *How to Internet*, 2012. Digital Video, screenshot.
http://www.jaakkopallasvuo.com/howto.html

"The boundless growth of apparatuses in our time corresponds to the equally extreme proliferation in processes of subjectification. This may produce the impression that in our time, the category of subjectivity is wavering and losing its consistency; but what is at stake, to be precise, is not an erasure or an overcoming, but rather a dissemination." —
Giorgio Agamben, What Is an Apparatus?

There is more to Internet art than mere design and aesthetics. It calls attention to the spatial reconstruction caused by the interface and subverts the habitual nature of technology's use, bearing significant implications for subjectivity. As we know, technology causes societal change on both macroscopic and individual levels. By failing to address these changes, we also fail to develop an informed attitude toward the changing nature of subjectivity. In particular, we fail to develop a sense of subjectivity that allows us to distinguish between mediated space and reality. Internet art (often referred to as "net art") prompts a reinterpretation of the network and, particularly, the interface. [1] Net art creates the conditions necessary for critical reflection by disassembling the elaborate technical ensemble of the interface into its smallest symbolic parts, and then reassembling them into a particular visual language. The work indicates a break, or disruption, from a procedural flow. [2] Net art promotes the interface's revelation of itself.

That said, it's critical to begin by examining the interface. The interface is an apparatus that affects the way its users perceive, acquire, and disseminate information, both online and offline. [3]With respect to computing, an interface is the program wherein we navigate software, hardware, or peripheral devices such as monitors and keyboards. "In semiotic terms, the computer interface acts as a code that carries cultural messages in a variety of media," notes new media theorist Lev Manovich. "The interface shapes how the computer user conceives of the computer itself. It also determines how users think of any media object accessed via a computer." [4] According to Manovich, the interface isn't merely a neutral part of the computing process; rather, it has the capacity to impose its own logic on media. "[F]ar from being a transparent window into the data inside a computer," Manovich writes, "the interface brings with it strong messages of its own." [5] These messages are the semiotic content of the interface, and they endow it with a cultural grammar. They carry a set of prescriptions about its use that, most often, go unnoticed.

Mobile devices, such as the cellular phone, laptop, and tablet, enable us to mediate through interfaces across many different environments. This is partly how the interface permeates every aspect of life, making all media aesthetics uncannily uniform. The interface is a program we traverse freely all the time, and yet, it seems invisible to us. Design consciously foretells a new ethos of personal computing, characterized by the disappearance of technology products as they fully coalesce into other objects, surfaces, and spaces.

The term "design," both a noun and a verb, derived from the Latin *signum* meaning "sign," has multiple definitions. Once we become aware of design as a construct, technology becomes demystified. It's actually strange when we consider the relationship of terms like design, technology, and machine; we begin to notice that their etymons all concern terms like cunning, fabrication, or artifice – to *de-sign*, essentially, reduces to the *removal* of a sign or symbol. [6] Czech media theorist Vilém Flusser writes at length about the technological image and its ability to change the way that we see the world. "A machine is a device designed to deceive;" he explains, "a lever, for example, cheats gravity." [7] When we consider it in this light, it becomes evident that design actually does require some degree of artifice. It could even be said that design has a tendency to deceive nature through technology – to replace the natural with the artificial. [8] Interacting through such a highly designed, highly artificial environment can radically shift everyday micro-behaviors, affecting autonomy and tactility at once. The interface acts, essentially, as a series of embedded deflections that prevent us from having any kind of perspective of the depth of time, putting us into a state of reaction almost constantly.

Just as twentieth-century modernism was determined by technologies of manufacturing, mass media and lens-based imagery, the most pressing condition determining contemporary culture may well be the omnipresence of the Internet. The Internet's reach was extended by the popularization of Web 2.0, a second-stage development of the World Wide Web characterized by shared information, user-generated content, and the emergence of social networking. [9] The Internet underpins the whole apparatus of communication and data processing by which our hyperconnected culture operates. Without it, we would have no email or chat software, no computer-aided industrial production, and none of the invisible, "smart" design-interfaces that we continually rely on.

It's become increasingly obvious that we have to approach our exchanges through web technology with some level of caution. To ignore this responsibility is to slip into a kind of magical thinking historically linked to "mythology." We have to question how it is we can actually connect with one another through a space of mythologized, technological immateriality – and how this myth has come to affect subjectivity and individual agency. Marshall McLuhan writes in his comprehensive study *Understanding Media*:

All technological extensions of ourselves must be numb and subliminal, else we could not endure the leverage exerted upon us by such extension... No society has ever known enough about its actions to have developed immunity to its new extensions or technologies. [10]

He warns, prophetically, that we are as much a product of our tools as they are of us; technology routinely outpaces our ability to locate or interrogate its effects.

The interface remains elusive because it is so difficult to determine its anti-environment, a term used by McLuhan to describe a separate vantage point from which to view an environment in which one is immersed. [11] A fish, for instance, is blithely unaware of the water surrounding it, as it has no anti-environment that would enable it to perceive the very element it lives in. The temptation of the fish is simply not to see the water, and thereby avoid acknowledging it. The lack of an anti-environment similarly removes the interface from view, leading the user to regard it, correctly, as something largely beyond comprehension. Interface invisibility contributes to a sense-distorting, technological bias that, in McLuhan's terms, has been accepted subliminally throughout most of modern history.

I begin this text by outlining the cultural inclination toward transparency throughout interface development. Moving forward, I discuss what Slovenian philosopher and cultural critic Slavoj Žižek calls "interpassivity." In his work, *The Plague of Fantasies*, Žižek uses the term to highlight the contradictory nature of using the word interactive to describe digital mediation. He regards so-called interactivity as an oversimplification of the user-interface dynamic. Interactivity assumes that the user is in dialogue with technology when, in fact, there is no dialogue, and no action on the user's part. [12] Instead, interpassivity describes the transposing of the user's emotion or attention onto another entity or object that consequently "acts" in his or her place. [13] Basically, the ubiquity of computing actively encourages the user's passive attitude toward reality.

I continue to discuss code language as a form of "magic," which subsequently guides the user's speculative imagination about computational power. I also explain the how the technical glitch, often read as a malfunction, or error, can be seen as a necessary and productive element for critique. I conclude by addressing at length how Internet artists invite malfunction, or manipulation, into their aesthetic practices, resulting in a reinterpretation of the interface and, perhaps, a revitalization of the avant-garde.

What is at stake in Internet art is not only what it produces but how it is produced. Although the terminology used to chronicle this work remains largely undeveloped, the discourse about how best to perceive web technology as a platform for the circulation of artwork is not new. Public astonishment surrounding the rise of computer networking in the late 1980s was coupled with an enthusiasm for dispersed authorship. Indeed, dispersed authorship and anonymity contributed to the preemptive exclusion of the Internet from the fine arts as a widely accepted medium for art practice. [14]

Nevertheless, in the early 1990s, Internet artists began to connect through the *Nettime* mailing list, developing novel methods for the production and exchange of their work. [15] The original "net. art" movement included an assembly of European and Russian net artists and writers. Among these artists were Heath Bunting, Vuk Ćosić, Jodi.org, Olia Lialina, and Alexei Shulgin, whose contributions and audiences remain almost exclusively online. The use of an online platform resulted in the long-term failure to document net art or, at least, to connect it to other art-historical practices. [16] In many cases, "net artists" relocated themselves to safer, more installation-based grounds as "media artists." This relocation essentially traded the web browser for the traditional gallery space.

Computer coding can be the force behind movement across digital space; it can even lead to the formation of images and three-dimensional objects. That said, the degree of code manipulation unique to network-based art ought to challenge our approach to the interface and enable a new perspective on computation altogether. For instance, Post-Internet art refers specifically to works that are consciously created with the assumption that the network's omnipresence is a given. The name refers to a set of assumptions rather than a time "after" the Internet. These assumptions indicate that the centrality and distribution of the network are passé — that the Internet is no longer a novelty, but a banality. [17] Post-Internet artwork employs much of the visual rhetoric of outdated Internet branding, stock imagery, and various technical glitches in order to highlight the ways a networked system functions and malfunctions. [18] Post-Internet art seems to celebrate the pastiche and near-obsolescence of early web technology in displays of anti-aestheticism and anti-design [*see fig. 1*].

The observations that follow are situated within media theory, which serves as a context for developing a critical canon of network-based art. They are largely concerned with the changing nature of subjectivity with respect to theoretically vanishing technologies. The discussion of works based on their relative technicity will have less import than the way this technicity reveals the interface in general. [19] The pervasive interface of the web provides ideal conditions for interpassivity, reconstructing the subject via media objects. Network-based art plays both a unique and necessary role in subverting the programmed nature of interface technology.

In fact, according to McLuhan, this sort of intervention is the singular ability of the artist, as the artist anticipates and responds to cultural and technological challenges well in advance of their effect:

The ordinary person seeks security by numbing his perception against the impact of new experience; the artist delights in this novelty and instinctively creates situations that reveal it and compensate for it. The artist puts on the distortion of sensory life produced by new environmental programming and creates artistic antidotes to correct the sensory derangement brought by the new form. [20]

Internet art can act as an antidote to interface mediation, one that might subvert cultural attitudes toward — and assumptions about — vanishing technologies.

Notes

[1] I often use the term "network-based art" in an attempt to condense the various terms circulating in current discourse about Internet-related art practices, among them: Net Art, Browser Art, Internet Art, the New Aesthetic, New Media, Post-media, Internet-Aware, and Post-Internet. Regardless of the term, network-based art practices require an Internet component or—at the very least—an awareness of Internet culture and communication. The most concise definition I've come across in my studies is that of critic Josephine Bosma in *Nettitudes: Let's Talk Net Art*. Net art, according to Bosma, is art based on Internet cultures, or within them, whether or not the works themselves are predominantly technological. See the glossary for extended definitions of Internet and net art related terms.

[2] See Rosa Menkman's *The Glitch Moment(um)* (Amsterdam: Institute of Network Cultures, 2011), 27. Menkman introduces the term "procedural" in reference to "procedural programming," which describes a series of computational steps that must be carried out in order for a program to reach a desired state.

[3] See Giorgio Agamben's *What Is an Apparatus? And Other Essays* (Stanford, CA: Stanford University Press, 2009), 14. Agamben expands on the Foucauldian apparatus, defining it as literally anything with the ability to capture, orient, determine, intercept, model, control, or secure the gestures, behaviors, opinions, or discourses of living beings.

[4] Lev Manovich, *The Language of New Media* (Cambridge, MA: The MIT Press, 2001).

[5] Ibid.

[6] Vilém Flusser, *The Shape of Things: A Philosophy of Design* (London: Reaktion

Books, 1999), 17—19.

[7] Ibid.

[8] Flusser, *The Shape of Things*, 17—19.

[9] Lev Manovich, "The Practice of Everyday (Media) Life: From Mass Consumption to Mass Cultural Production," *Critical Inquiry 35*, no. 2 (Winter 2009), 319, accessed December 3, 2013, http://www.jstor.org/stable/10.1086/596645. "Web 2.0" was coined by Tim O'Reilly in 2004. It refers to the use of commercially developed social platforms in contrast to the network of individual, amateur home pages that dominated the web before its development. Important concepts for Web 2.0 include user-generated content, long-tail, network as platform, syndication, and mass collaboration.

[10] Marshall McLuhan, *Understanding Media: the Extensions of Man* (Cambridge, MA: The MIT Press, 1994), 64.

[11] Marshall McLuhan and Quentin Fiore, *War and Peace in the Global Village* (Berkeley: Gingko Press, 2001), 175.

[12] Slavoj Žižek, *The Plague of Fantasies* (London: Verso, 1997), 112—116.

[13] Ibid.

[14] Bosma, *Nettitudes: Let's Talk Net Art* (Rotterdam: NAi Publishers, 2011), 65.

[15] Josephine Bosma, "Is It a Commercial? Noooo...Is It Spam? Nooo...It Is Net Art!" Josephine Bosma, accessed November 11, 2013, http://www.josephinebosma.com/web/node/46.

[16] Rachel Greene, *Internet Art* (New York: Thames & Hudson, 2004), 19.

[17] Gene McGugh, *Post Internet* (Brescia: LINK Editions, 2011), 5.

[18] Retromediation is, conceivably, the deliberate return to an earlier form of media for the very material qualities of production that such a medium possesses.

[19] Bosma, *Nettitudes*, 25. Technicity is a term introduced by French philosopher Gilbert Simondon. It was recently employed by Adrian MacKenzie in *Transductions: Bodies and Machines at Speed*, to describe the varying levels of cultural complexity with regard to tools and technology.

[20] Marshall McLuhan and Harley Parker, *Through the Vanishing Point: Space in Poetry and Painting* (New York: Harper & Row, 1968), 237— 38.

1.0
Transparency

Fig. 2 Jeremy Strathman, *Untitled 2013*. Collage.
http://internetpoetry.tumblr.com/post/61984103665

"Giedion, Mendelssohn, and Le Corbusier turned the abiding place of man into a transit area for every conceivable kind of energy and for electric currents and radio waves. The time that is coming will be dominated by transparency." — Walter Benjamin, The Return of the Flâneur

There's no such thing as a simple interface. Despite the seemingly straightforward appearance of images and text on various programs, the interface is usually preceded by complex data processing and hidden support systems. Today, it's almost inevitable for us to regard interfaces in terms of our familiarity with the web page. In doing so, we extend its definition to include more novel concepts of computing such as mobile web browsing and applications (otherwise known as "apps").

Lev Manovich details Apple's 1984 development of the virtual page as a critical point of development in interface history. This graphical user interface (GUI) presented information within overlapping windows that were analogous to a set of book pages. "The user was given the ability to go back and forth between these pages as well as to scroll through individual pages," Manovich writes. "In this way, a traditional page was redefined as a virtual page, a surface which can be much larger than the limited surface of a computer screen." [1] This extended surface engendered a critical transformation of physical space — a collapse of space, as the late Jean Baudrillard might call it. Baudrillard uses the word "obscene" to describe the collapse of space through which we might view or interpret reality due in part to its mediated proximity. [2]

More specifically, his use of the word divides it into "ob-" (meaning "against") and "scene" (meaning "stage"). For Baudrillard, it is *obscene* precisely because it lacks a symbolic dimension, and the world without symbolism is a vulgar one. If the collapse of space via technology has resulted in a loss of symbolism, it's because technology has interfered with our ability to assign *meaning* to various concepts and symbols.

Even in the history of early electronic mailing systems, sending a message with a computer evoked the illusion of transparent communication within a space. Two people who are connected through a multilayered digital network can only access a single facet of the broader technical setup required to make the connection possible. When users communicate with each other online, the sense of distance collapses the moment a connection occurs. The text is both present and distant; it appears on the screen while simultaneously having reached its destination. This form of transparency is what distinguishes telematics from other forms of mediation. It is space without distance; it is communication wherein the medium appears unmediated.

The space beyond the screen has been colloquially termed "cyberspace," "virtual space," "global village," or "virtual sphere," among other metaphors for topological readings of the Internet. Again, the work of Baudrillard provides a provocative conceptual lens for discussing the figurative nature of the Internet as a cybernetic space. In "The Ecstasy of Communication," he warns that the absolute proximity of space easily moves us from a state of reflection and transcendence, to a state of complacence and pure communication. "Today the scene and mirror no longer exist," Baudrillard writes; "instead there is a screen and network. In place of the reflexive transcendence of mirror and scene, there is a nonreflecting surface, an immanent surface where operations unfold — the smooth operational surface of communication." [3] The conditions that he describes are found nowhere more prevalently than the Internet and the network that supports it.

Conceived initially as a governmental project called ARPANET, after the Department of Defense Agency that sponsored its development, the Internet was designed as a communication system that would be immune to nuclear attack. [4] Although the terms World Wide Web and Internet are so often used interchangeably, they don't actually refer to the same thing. Developed by Tim Berners-Lee and Robert Cailliau, the World Wide Web emerged as a single service on the Internet in 1989. [5] The two proposed a global hypertext markup language (HTML), a hypertext transfer protocol (HTTP), and a system of unique identifiers known as uniform resource locators (URLs) to implement a graphic web browser. [6] Parallel to the web's internal development, the Internet became a popular hobbyist and community venue, effectively decentralized and freed from physical constraints or locality. But exhaustive assimilation into Baudrillard's screen-space did not manifest until the move to Web 2.0 in the 2000s. [7]

On the early web browser, each webpage was a standalone destination. Although it existed in a networked space, its functional components remained self-contained and static. Early browsers prioritized specificity and publication rather than interoperability. As a result, each function remained separate: information was displayed in the browser as text; images and music were downloaded; and communication was relegated to email or chat software. Inevitable malfunctions resulted from inconsistent code rendering, proprietary software, and competing web standards. This was amended in the transition to Web 2.0, with its emphasis on information sharing. Content began to unify. Metaphorically speaking, it became less like a filing cabinet and more like us. [8] With the advent of data streaming came the transmission of media in the form of audio or video files as well as the further development of feedback, tagging, blogging, and content-management systems. The introduction of "WYSIWYG" (What You See Is What You Get) editing allowed users to contribute web content without having to write their own codes. [9] Web 2.0 is now characterized by a number of technical, cultural, and economic changes associated with the collective experience of the Internet. [10]

On a practical level, this experience was made possible by expanded bandwidths and larger storage capacities, as well as open-source web platforms and affordable software tools. These features allow users to both share media, and access media shared by others with ease. [11] This is precisely what marks the change between media and *social* media. [12] The container concept of "social media" is too often employed as a vague descriptor of loosely connected users on popular websites or mobile applications like Facebook, YouTube, Twitter, Wikipedia, and Instagram. My intention here is not to provide an in-depth analysis of the effects of social media but, rather, to call attention to a notion that has hitherto not been expressed about image cultures on the web — namely, that net artists can intuit an understanding of the web as a vastly influential apparatus that now impedes both our social and interior lives.

The term social media largely refers to online communities in the form of lists and forums; however, it acts instead as a reanimation of the social as simulacrum — a mere semblance of the social's ability to foster human relations imbued with meaning. Browsing or scrolling through global networks in cyberspace, we invest less time and energy in roles such as family, neighborhood, and marketplace. Once defined as citizens or members of a social class possessing certain rights, subjects are transformed into dynamic actors called "users." The "social" in social media no longer refers to society. Social networking appears to have more to do with the evolution of a single, cybernetic subject seeking to know itself in a field of the multitudes comprising its other. [13] Baudrillard contends that the subject is transformed neither by separation nor disconnection but by the instantaneous nature of total connection:

What characterizes him [the contemporary subject] is less the loss of the real, the light years of estrangement from the real, the pathos of distance and radical separation, as it is commonly said: but, very much to the contrary, the absolute proximity, the total instantaneity of things, the feeling of no defense, no retreat. It is the end of interiority and inti-

macy, the overexposure and transparence of the world which traverses
him without obstacle. He can no longer produce the limits of his own
being, can no longer stage himself, can no longer produce himself as
mirror. He is now only a pure screen, a switching center for all the
networks of influence. [14]

Baudrillard very clearly emphasizes the threat that instantaneity and transparency can bear on self-awareness and experience. Suffice it to say, the fact that the designs of computing products (among them laptops, desktop computers, iPhones, iPads, and accompanying power cables) have assumed such a seamless, minimal aesthetic should be suspect.

The recent surge of mobile web access has already displaced the computer model prevalent in the desktop era. [15] The unique characteristics of the mobile experience, with its compressed screen proportions and highly specialized icons, cause both interfaces and user-flows to become streamlined and uncomplicated. This design aesthetic indicates that the "object-hood" of technology ought to disappear; this is where we enter the era of imperceptibility.

The idea of a seamless, or transparent, infrastructure is addressed in this text specifically as it pertains to information culture. [16] Seamlessness denotes the dematerialization or "making inconspicuous" of a variety of ways that spaces and entities present information — traffic lights, flight and vehicle displays, on-screen menus, TV news layouts, magazines, e-readers, books, the interior design of commercial and leisure spaces such as banks and hotels and, principally, the interfaces of computer operating systems, software applications, and webpages. Seamless design deliberately disguises margins and transitional moments between various parts in order to present an ostensibly consistent or so-called interactive interface to

Fig. 3 Apple Advertisement for iOS 7, 2013. Screenshot.
http://www.apple.com/ios/design/
Fig. 4 Google Glass Advertisement, 2013. Screenshot.
https:/ www.youtube.com/watch?v=4EvNxWhskf8/

users. [17] A transparent interface is one without seams, one that its user can neither detect nor notice.

The redesign of Apple's mobile operating system, iOS 7, contained a full-scale removal of its formerly skeuomorphic elements, substituting them with an abstract concept of lightness, simplicity, and purity: "The interface is purposely unobtrusive," promised Apple's web advertisement, "Conspicuous ornamentation has been stripped away." [18] Perhaps the invisible interface par excellence, quite recently, was Google Glass [*see fig. 4*]. Google's optical, head-mounted display seamlessly integrated the functionality of digital computing. Technology was transformed into a superimposed, ubiquitous layer, and the data was abstracted away, reduced to storage management in "the cloud." [19] The sheer invisibility of Google Glass formed part of its problem: the device was supposed to bring technology closer to our senses, but, consequently, further distanced us from the physical world. [20]

Thinner, more compressed screens equipped with sophisticated data management capabilities are the quintessence of the vanishing interface. Seamless design strategies provoke a particular attitude toward the immaterial. French philosopher Jean-François Lyotard once claimed that the immaterial is not simply the opposite of matter itself, but rather a form of material extension that lives beyond direct human access. "The good old matter itself comes to us in the end as something which has been dissolved and reconstructed into complex formulas," he writes. "Reality consists of elements, organized by structural rules (matrices) in no longer human measures of space and time." [21] The information that floods our sensory environment via data storage systems, holograms, and computer programs is now comprised of such "soft"-ware that it is difficult (if not impossible) to measure. [22] It is at once intangible and located, and yet infinitely reproducible.

As data multiplies, it becomes less feasible for it to be regulated in terms that are accessible, or knowable, to most. The process of extracting order and pattern from the data of our online activity is rarely actualized by the common user. Instead, data handling is managed through complex tracking and aggregation techniques, whose status as the property of major corporations and institutions often remains concealed. [23] Walter Benjamin was once optimistic about the transparency of new forms of glass architecture — he saw it as a symbolic gesture for social and cultural truths. [24] But no longer do just light waves filter through glass — they're now accompanied by this incessant, albeit transparent, current of electromagnetic waves.

Depending on its context, the definition of transparency can refer either to visibility or invisibility. The former regards simplicity and clarity as a matter of view-ability, or even revelation. However, in interface technology, transparency means just the opposite — that is to say — invisibility and concealment. Information infrastructures, whether inconceivably small or inconceivably distant, simply can't be detected with the naked human eye. Satellites, for instance, are far too remote to be seen from Earth. And even what we view on a web interface as patterns, images, and text includes only the *perceptible* end of data. To make something perceptible as a data visualization means only that you've made it recognizable, which is not in the least similar to actually *perceiving* a thing. [25]

It is at the level of design that these new technologies become so problematic. The interface is not simply a piece of hardware concealing obscure, "immaterial" data structures; it is the surface at which we are made to mediate with this digital realm. In any case, the apparent seamlessness of technology may produce submissive attitudes in users and work to reorient subjectivity in general. The fantasy of transparency encourages users to feel as though they're interacting with technology, when they're simply immersed in a spectacle of constant mediation. This is part of the concept behind Žižekian interpassivity — to explain how some objects seemingly provide for own reception.

Notes

[1] Manovich, *The Language of New Media*, 84.
[2] Jean Baudrillard. "The Ecstasy of Communication," in *The Anti-Aesthetic: Essays on Postmodern Culture*, ed. Hal Foster (Seattle, WA: Bay Press, 1995), 125—133.
[3] Baudrillard, "The Ecstasy of Communication", 127.
[4] Greene, *Internet Art*, 18.
[5] Ibid.
[6] Ibid, 19.
[7] Manovich, "The Practice of Everyday (Media) Life", 319.
[8] Anthony Antonellis, *Impulse 101: An Essay about Art, the Internet, and Everything* (master's thesis, Bauhaus — Universität Weimar, 2011), 27.
[9] Denis Howe, "What You See Is What You Get," *FOLDOC*, March 3, 1999, accessed December 10, 2013, http://foldoc.org/WYSIWYG. WYSIWYG is an acronym for What You See Is What You Get, which is used to describe a computing method where the content entered on screen corresponds directly with the display manner in which it will be output.
[10] Manovich, "The Practice of Everyday (Media) Life", 319.
[11] Ibid.
[12] Adrian Chan, "Social Media: Paradigm Shift?", in *Gravity7*, http://www.gravity7.com/paradigm_shift_1 .html, accessed December 11, 2013.
[13] David Crawford, *Art and the Real-Time Archive: Remix, Relocation, Response*, 79. http://www.turbulence.org/studios/crawford/art_and_the_real_time_archive.pdf, accessed December 11, 2013
[14] Baudrillard, "The Ecstasy of Communication", 133.
[15] James O'Toole, "Mobile Apps Overtake Pc Internet Usage in U.S.," *CNN*,

February 28, 2014, accessed March 24, 2014, http://money.cnn.com/2014/02/28/technology/mobile/mobile-apps-internet.

[16] Lev Manovich, *The Language of New Media*, 13. Information culture describes how different cultural sites and objects present information to users.

[17] Lev Manovich, *The Language of New Media*, 13.

[18] "Why Apple Ditched Its Skeuomorphic Design for iOS7," *The Guardian*, http://www.theguardian.com/technology/shortcuts/2013/jun/12/skeuomorphism-apple-ditched-ios7, accessed December 14, 2013. See also "Apple—iOS7—Design," *Apple*, http://www.apple.com/ios/design/ accessed December 14, 2013. iOS is a mobile operating system distributed by Apple Inc., used on Apple devices such as the iPhone and iPad series. Skeuomorphism refers to a design principle in which design cues are taken from the physical world. The term is frequently applied to user interfaces, where much of the design aims to recall the real world — such as the use of folder and files images for computer filing systems, or a envelope symbols for email.

[19] Ian Bogost, "Google Zombie: The Glass Wearers of Tomorrow," *The Atlantic*, May 20, 2013. http://www.theatlantic.com/technology/archive/2013/05/google-zombie-the-glass-wearers-of-tomorrow/276007/, accessed December 12, 2013.

[20] Ibid.

[21] Bruce W. Ferguson, Reesa Greenberg, and Sandy Nairne, eds., *Thinking about Exhibitions* (London: Routledge, 1996), 159.

[22] Flusser, *The Shape of Things*, 87.

[23] Anna Munster, *Networked: A (networked_book) about (networked_art)*, accessed December 12, 2013, http://munster.networkedbook.org.

[24] Walter Benjamin, "A Small History of Photography," in *Walter Benjamin: One Way Street and Other Writings*, trans. Edmund Jephcott and Kingsley Shorter (London: Verso, 1985), 240 — 257.

[25] Munster, *Networked*.

2.0

Interpassivity;
Or,
Consequences
of the
Extended Self

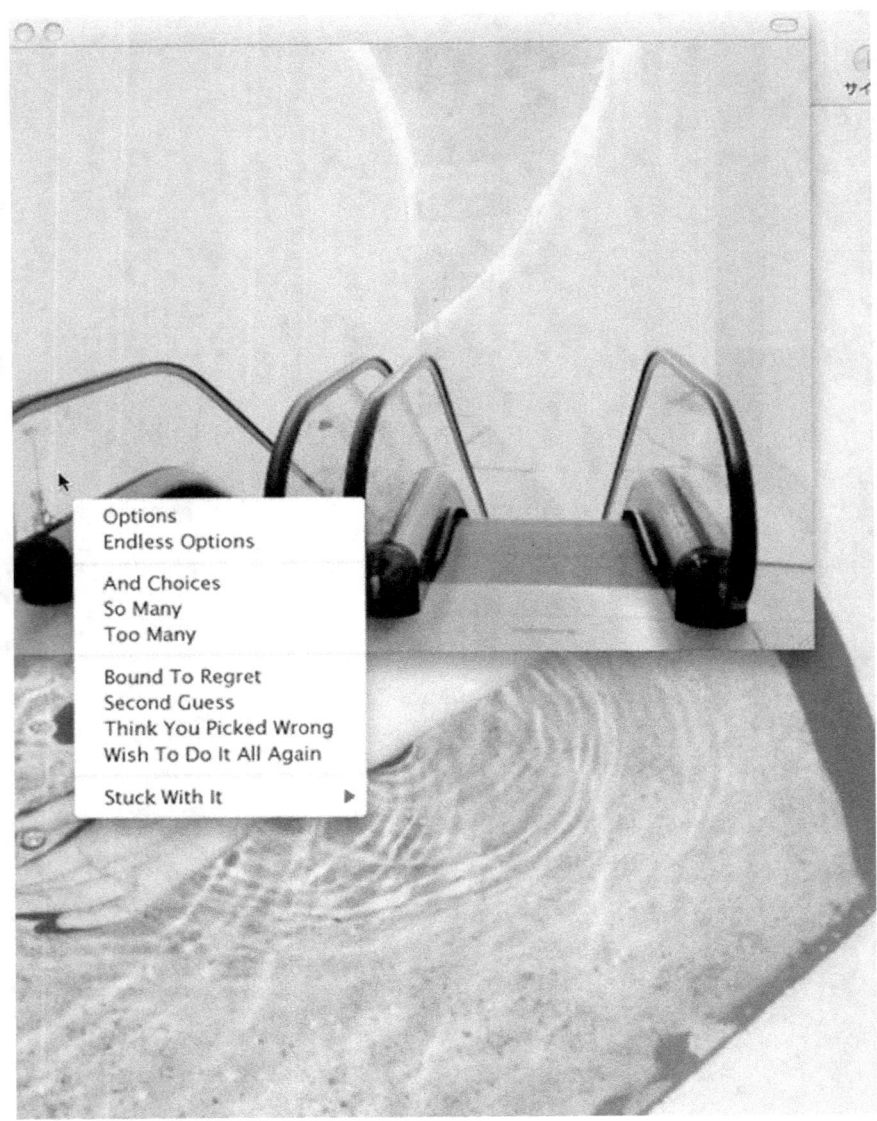

Options
Endless Options

And Choices
So Many
Too Many

Bound To Regret
Second Guess
Think You Picked Wrong
Wish To Do It All Again

Stuck With It   ▶

Fig. 5. Roseanna M. Africa, *Untitled*, 2013. Screenshot.
http://ramswork.com/screencaptures_volume2.html

"Virtuality comes close to happiness only because it surreptitiously removes all reference to things. It gives you everything, but at the same time it subtly deprives you of everything. The subject is realized to perfection, but when realized to perfection, the subject automatically becomes object, and panic sets in." — Baudrillard, Screened Out

Not only has the fantasy of achieving a transparent interface changed the way people relate to machines, it's also morphed some of our very basic notions of human subjectivity and, subsequently, human experience. What German theorist Hans Ulrich Gumbrecht terms "subject-effects" are produced by this fundamental relation between humans and technology:

Couplings between human bodies, psychic systems, and new communications technologies... produce specific subject-effects. With this perspective, they diverge from a historiographical tradition that describes technical innovations as motivated by collective needs and as "invented" by subjective genius. Instead of confirming the deeply rooted belief in an instrumental relation between the subject and different technologies, they encourage us to experiment with the inversion of this narrative pattern. [1]

Gumbrecht asserts that innovation is no longer driven by collective needs, and addressed by subjective genius, but driven by singular needs and then invented by collective genius. This inversion of the typical "narrative pattern" that sees "technical innovations," he suggests, is that technology now has the ability to determine subjectivity, rather than subjectivity inventing, or producing, technology.

Žižek's concept of interpassivity is a sound basis for understanding these sorts of subject-effects. Although the terms used to discuss these effects are many, they will not all be addressed at length here. In his highly influential essay "What is an Apparatus?," for instance, Italian philosopher Giorgio Agamben argues that subjectivity would appear to be wavering, or disappearing, when it is in fact disseminating — dispersing throughout the networks. [2] This seems to be the consensus among most media theorists and artists writing on the topic. For Roy Ascott, subjectivity is no longer localized in a single point in space or time, rather, it is distributed through networks. For Siegfried Zielinski, subjectivity is the possibility of action at the frontier of networks. For Pierre Lévy, subjectivity has become fractal. [3] Neil Postman goes so far as saying that technology changes what it means to be human: "It undermines certain mental processes and social relations that make life worth living." [4] A uniting feature of this theoretical landscape is sensory derangement, in McLuhan's sense of the term: the destruction of the nature of our fundamental, sensorial experience. Interpassivity expresses the capacity of technology to consume us, even as we consume it. In this sense, technology isn't only an outward extension of ourselves, but also an inward projection.

Interpassivity is the act of projecting one's subjective emotion, or activity, onto an outside entity, or object, which subsequently "acts" in one's place, or stead. As conceptualized by Žižek, interpassivity denotes the manner in which media objects complete the role normally assumed by the spectator, even to the extent of accomplishing the act of enjoyment for him. [5] The spectator is made a bystander; his involvement in the realization of the media is rendered superfluous, effectively *decentering* him from within. While "interactivity" remains the catchphrase of contemporary digital technology, it's become an increasingly inadequate description of our actual experience with the screen. The cultural temptation is to emphasize the democratic principle of technology — the new possibility for people to break free from the role of "passive observer" and participate more actively in the spectacle unfolding before them. But Žižek questions what is dialogic about the relationship between observer and spectacle:

Is, however, the other side of this interactivity not interpassivity? Is the necessary obverse of my interacting with the object instead of just passively following the show, not the situation in which the object itself takes from me, deprives me of, my own passive reaction of satisfaction (or mourning or laughter), so that is is the object itself which "enjoys the show" instead of me, relieving me of the superego duty to enjoy myself.

Zizek's description nearly echoes the concept of the surrogate self presented by Lacan in his deliberation over the chorus in Greek tragedy: "The chorus expressed the terror and compassion felt by the audience, who were apparently pleased to be relieved of such psychological stress." [6] The affective response to the theatre is thereby performed by a "surrogate self"— the chorus — as the appropriate emotive response to the performance. A surrogate self acts as a substitute for the subject. "[T]he emotional commentary is done for you," demonstrating that even one's "most intimate feelings can be radically externalised [*sic*]." [7]

The contradictory nature of "interactivity" has also been examined by Espen Aarseth, principal researcher at the Center for Computer Games Research at the IT University at Copenhagen. Aarseth

argues that the term "ergodic," a combination of Greek etymons meaning *work* and *path*, actually better communicates the labyrinthine trajectory that a user traverses through a given virtual space. [8] He writes about interactivity as "a purely ideological term, projecting an unfocused fantasy rather than a concept of any analytical significance." [9] While interactivity recognizes autonomy and participation as general principles of social recognition, interpassivity indicates how the stress produced by this promise merely encourages acquiescence. In a 1996 post distributed via *Nettime*, early net.artist Alexei Shulgin comments on this paradox of so-called interactivity in the realm of new media art:

Looking at very popular media art form such as "interactive installation" I always wonder how people (viewers) are excited about this new way of manipulation on them. It seems that manipulation is the only form of communication they know and can appreciate. They are happily following very few options given to them... press left or right button, jump or sit... But what nice words you can hear around it: interaction, interface for self-expression, artificial intelligence, communication even [sic]. [10]

For Shulgin, new forms of manipulation are simply paraded under the guise of "interactive" media. Media acquisitions only entail the end of enjoyment, and the beginning of manipulation.

For instance, we might record television programs without getting the chance to watch them; the television, as it were, views the program on our behalf. Again, Žižek analyzes this phenomenon:

Let us remind ourselves of a phenomenon quite usual in popular television shows or serials: 'canned laughter'. After some supposedly funny or witty remark, you can hear the laughter and applause included in the soundtrack of the show itself. So even if, tired from a hard day's

stupid work, all evening we did nothing but gaze drowsily into the te-
levision screen, we can say afterwards that objectively, through the
medium of the other, we had a really good time. [11]

If the medium, that is, the mediator of subject-effects, receives
or "enjoys" media in our place, one might conclude that it is no
longer necessary to enjoy ourselves; and that our involvement only
sustains the activity of the medium. We've become so desensiti-
zed by the overstimulation of images and information that we only
require yet more doses of stimulation. What becomes prevalent is
the sheer quantity of circulation itself. Ironically, what begins to
typify this form of expedited dissemination is the uncannily static.
Alongside every banal compulsion is yet another interruption. What
we enjoy, actually, is the protection by the machine that stands in
for our own subjectivity. Entertainment is always mediation, and
always, essentially, involved in the process of subjectification. The
idea that technologies alter subjects (i.e. produce subject-effects)
has long been tied to the idea of the compliant observer following
the spectacle staged by others.

Interpassivity points out the prominent role of media in general,
especially their ability to redirect our attention away from superfi-
cial constructions. Purposeful action is radically refashioned as a
result of preprogrammed technology. What we arrive at instead is a
series of simple modifications based on a set of rules dictated by a
program; the user remains a user.

Notes

[1] Hans Ulrich Gumbrecht and K. Ludwig Pfeiffer, eds., "A Farewell to Interpretation," in *Materialities of Communication* (Stanford, CA: Stanford University Press, 1994), 400—401.

[2] Agamben, *What Is an Apparatus?*, 15.

[3] Edmond Couchot, "The Automatization of Figurative Techniques: Towards the Autonomous Image," in *Media Art Histories*, ed. Oliver Grau (Cambridge, MA: MIT Press, 2007), 183.

[4] Neil Postman, *Technopoly: The Surrender of Culture to Technology* (New York: Vintage, 1993), xii.

[5] Žižek, *The Plague of Fantasies*, 111.

[6] Jacques Lacan, *The Seminar of Jaques Lacan: The Ethics of Psychoanalysis* (London: Routledge, 1992), 252.

[7] Ibid.

[8] Espen J. Aarseth, *Cybertext: Perspectives on Ergodic Literature* (Baltimore: Johns Hopkins University Press, 1997), 48—51.

[9] Ibid., 51.

[10] Alexei Shulgin, "Art Power and Communication," *Nettime*, October 7, 1996, http://amsterdam.nettime.org/Lists-Archives/nettime-l-9610/msg00036.html. Accessed May 16, 2014.

[11] Slavoj Žižek, *The Sublime Object of Ideology* (London: Verso, 1997).

3.0
"In the Beginning was the Command Line"

"With its seeming opacity and the boundless, viral multiplication of its output in the execution, algorithmic code opens up a vast potential for cultural imagination, phantasms and phantasmagorias. The word made flesh, writing taking up a life of its own by self-execution, has been a utopia and dystopia in religion, metaphysics, art, and techno-logy alike." — Florian Cramer, Words Made Flesh: Code, Culture, Imagination

The command line has replaced the logos. The symbols of code language have the power to manipulate the interface, performing variable actions across computer networks. In his book *Words Made Flesh: Code, Culture, Imagination*, German theorist Florian Cramer writes about the magical premise underlying the idea that language can affect the physical realm. Admittedly, this idea is not new, as the beginning of the Gospel of John in the New Testament makes clear:

1:1 In the beginning was the Word, and the Word was with God, and the Word was God.
1:14 And the Word was made flesh, and dwelt among us, (and we beheld his glory, the glory as of the only begotten of the Father,) full of grace and truth.

The word made flesh, that is to say, the idea of language as a pro-ducer of vital and multiple concrete effects, finds new precedence in computer programming.

In theory, the images and text viewable on a computer screen are identical, or somehow reducible, to the symbols of the program-ming languages that store, manipulate, and display them. The inter-face enables a form of communication, whether that form is purely algorithmic (as in the famous binary code consisting of zeroes and ones) or visually interoperable at the level of web browsing. [1]

Physical traits are often projected onto the machine: when it stops functioning, it's said to "die." One can put a computer to "sleep." [2] We even attribute "memory" to the machine. The history of human language is both complicated and enriched by all of these additional layers. Programming language communicates a set of instructions to machines, particularly to computers. It can be used to create programs or media objects, or to control the operation of the computer, effectively moving a language from the realm of symbol and metaphor to that of real, performative potential. Cramer claims that programming finds a historical precedent in alchemy: "The technical principle of magic, controlling matter through manipulation of symbols, is the technical principle of computer software as well." [3]

It's unsurprising that magic might manifest itself in software, at least figuratively. In a so-called immaterial culture, that is to say, a culture in which information is transmitted through the electromagnetic field, the program is tantamount to the data that comprises it. [4] In *The Shape of Things*, Flusser connects the original opposition of matter and form (i.e., container and contained) to the design of computer programs and communication networks:

All eternal forms, all immutable Ideas, can be formulated as equations, and these equations can be translated from the numerical code into computer codes and fed into computers. The computer for its part can display these algorithms as lines, areas and (a bit later on) volumes on the screen and in holograms, out of which it can create 'numerically generated' artificial images. [5]

Paradoxically, though, these immutable forms *can* change: one can distort, twist, shrink, and enlarge them. [6] To alter media and produce variable images out of symbols and codes manifests as a form of real (i.e., realizable) magic. In fact, any amount of sufficiency in computing can be compared to a magic. Cultural critic Lee Siegel suggests a major difference in his study *Net of Magic: Wonders of India*:

> *"I'm writing a book on magic," I explain, and I'm asked, "Real magic?" By* real magic *people mean miracles, thaumaturgical acts, and supernatural powers. "No," I answer: "Conjuring tricks, not real magic."* Real magic, *in other words, refers to the magic that is not real, while the magic that is real, that can actually be done, is* not real magic. [7]

Combined, the reliability and invisibility of computer technology amount to a form of magic that can "actually be done." References to magic already abound in computer software branding, from the assumed benevolence and upward bias of the storage "cloud" to the program genre of "Setup Wizards." User attitudes toward technology are influenced, if not guided, by this sort of language. Broader divides between code and user perception lead to broader, more speculative, ideas about the machine. [8]

The dematerialization of technology is analyzed in depth by N. Katherine Hayles in her essay "Virtual Bodies and Flickering Signifiers." She discusses the proclivity for the immaterial as evidence of an inclination towards pattern and randomness:

> *[T]he contemporary pressure toward dematerialization, understood as an epistemic shift toward pattern/randomness and away from presence/absence, affects human and textual bodies on two levels at once, as a change in the body (the material substrate) and a change in the message (the codes of representation). [9]*

For Hayles, the problem of immateriality is framed by this sort of epistemic shift. Information technologies not only change modes of text production, storage, and dissemination; they also transform the relationship between signified and signifier. She proposes a new, or emergent, object, one that she dubs a "flickering signifier":

> *In informatics, the signifier can no longer be understood as a single marker, for example an ink mark on a page. Rather it exists as a flexible chain of markers bound together by the arbitrary relations specified by the relevant codes. As I write these words on my computer, I see the lights on the video screen, but for the computer, the relevant signifiers are magnetic tracks on disks. Intervening between what I see and what the computer reads are the machine code [sic] that correlates alphanumeric symbols with binary digits, the compiler language that correlates these symbols with higher-level instructions determining how the symbols are to be manipulated, the processing program that mediates between these instructions and the commands I give the computer, and so forth. A signifier on one level becomes a signified on the next-higher level. [10]*

The relationship between "signifiers" and "signifieds" at each level can be changed with a single command; this relationship is possible because what is reproduced through a code language is pattern rather than presence. "The longer the chain of codes," Hayles continues, "the more radical the transformations that can be affected. Acting as linguistic levers, chains of code can impart astonishing power with even very small changes." [11]

Much like magical symbols, Hayles' flickering signifier is characterized by unpredictable metamorphoses and dispersions. It finds precedence in Lacan's "floating signifier," which she reads as an analytic metaphor applied to language borne by a delivery medium (i.e. print). [12] But Hayles' "flickering signifiers" are literally "flickering" because the medium has become screenic. The text seems to exist elsewhere, through the glaring window of the interface rather than on the page itself. The "power" of structured chains of code relies on the fact that manipulations of the command line can catalyze massively cascading effects. These effects constitute a form of power in the now-familiar technological sense — the power to alter the behavior of a system.

It's worth reiterating that the interface itself is a complex programmable entity whose structure includes, in many cases, an underlying textual command line. The command line is a point of potential for artistic intervention. Working with code or computing as an artistic, or poetic, endeavor entails the revelation of underlying, imperceptible, perhaps even concealed structures of control and, thus, serves a genuinely subversive function. [13] Which begets this question: if Internet art can alter the behavior of a networked system, does it, too, constitute a form of power?

Notes

[1] Bosma, *Nettitudes: Let's Talk Net Art*, 66.

[2] Ibid., 100.

[3] Cramer, *Words Made Flesh*, 15.

[4] Flusser, *The Shape of Things*, 24.

[5] Ibid., 41.

[6] Ibid., 42.

[7] Lee Siegel, *Net of Magic: Wonders and Deceptions in India* (Chicago: University of Chicago Press, 1991), 425.

[8] Cramer, *Words Made Flesh*, 8.

[9] N. Katherine Hayles, "Virtual Bodies and Flickering Signifiers," in *Electronic Culture: Technology and Visual Representation* (New York: Aperture Foundation, 1996), 262.

[10] Ibid., 264.

[11] Ibid.

[12] Ibid., 263. Lacan wished to deny any one-to-one correspondence between the signifier and the signified. Hayles contends that in something like word processing; however, language is code.

[13] Florian Cramer, "Digital Code and Literary Text," *netzliteratur.net*, accessed May 13, 2014, http://www.netzliteratur.net/cramer/digital_code_and_literary_text.html.

4.0
The Function of the Malfunction

"Malfunction and failure are not signs of improper production. On the contrary, they indicate the active production of the "accidental potential" in any product. The invention of the ship implies its wreckage, the steam engine and the locomotive discover the derailment."
— *Paul Virilio,* The Art of the Accident

The so-termed "glitch aesthetic" employed by many network-based artists poses both a technological and perceptual challenge to convention. The glitch can modulate and reshape the norms of an interface-mediated space. In the words of Dutch theorist Rosa Menkman, a glitch is a break from the conventional flow of digital information that results in a perceived accident or error. [1] Or put simply, a glitch disrupts expected functionality. "Glitch, an unexpected occurrence, unintended result, or break or disruption in a system, cannot be singularly codified," Menkman writes, "which is precisely its conceptual strength and dynamical contribution to media theory." [2]

Developers often design technology to encourage the user to forget about the presence of the medium. When we consider the complexity of the user's aesthetic and perceptual relationship to the interface, it's apparent that user engagement would require a much more stimulating approach. Art historian Ernst Gombrich observes that an excessive imposition of rules often leads to monotony, producing little deviation or excitement. "However we analyse the difference between the regular and the irregular, we must ultimately be able to account for the most basic fact of aesthetic experience," he writes, "the fact that delight lies somewhere between boredom and confusion." [3] It turns out that the richness of a media experience can't depend on extreme immediacy or reliability. In many cases, users require an exchange between surprise and uniformity to remain actively engaged. [4] Expanding on this important role of irregularity and surprise in human perception, Menkman examines the glitch as a necessary interruption from a technological flow, often followed by a feeling of momentary shock, loss, or awe. [5]

The processes and codes underlying any given interface are presented as clean, flattened landscapes of cascading windows and floating icons. When such a flow breaks, the user bears witness to the very data functions they habitually rely on, but do not typically see. This demystification prompts a momentary void of meaning; technological interruptions are perceived as alarming or uncanny. But these interruptions also cause the user to reflect critically, for instance, upon the meaning of said interruption. [6] Media theorist Eric Kluitenberg discusses the reflection motivated by technological interruption. He observes a particular reaction on September 11, 2001, when the CNN website temporarily malfunctioned and a black screen repeatedly interfered the flow of its television broadcast: "the rupture of professional media codes, which signaled complete panic and disarray... the infinity of possible alternative discourses, of other possible modes of explanation and interpretation." [7]

As Kluitenberg suggests, part of what the glitch challenges is the idea of authorship itself. Prior to this voiding moment, the role of the author is neutralized from the entire mediated experience. The seamless surface of the networked media spectacle, and its illusion of stability, obscures any sense of authorship whatsoever. [8] Technological glitches disrupt those illusions, opening the interface to a space of the unknown — that which cannot be described, explained, or planned for. It is the moment at which this flow is interrupted that a counter-experience becomes possible. When the sound has collapsed and the screen has faded, the possibility for an alternative message unfolds. Through the distorted lens of the glitch, a viewer can perceive images of machinic inputs and outputs. The interface no longer behaves the way it is programmed to; the uncanny encounter with a glitch produces a new mode that confounds an otherwise predictable masquerade of human-computer relations. [9]

Notions of disaster, failure, and accident have long been integral to the progression of avant-garde and contemporary art. With the rising centrality of technology, the accident becomes vital to culture, as Paul Virilio has emphasized most strongly among media theorists:

To invent the sailing ship or steamer is to invent the shipwreck. *To invent the train is* to invent the rail accident *of derailment. To invent the family automobile is to produce the* pile-up *on the highway. To get what is heavier than air to take off in the form of an aeroplane or dirigible is* to invent the crash, *the air disaster. As for the space shuttle,* Challenger, *its blowing up in flight in the same year that the tragedy of Chernobyl occurred is the* original accident *of a new motor, the equivalent of the first ship-wreck of the very first ship. [10]*

Virilio argues that although people are inclined to interpret accidents as negative experiences or failures, they can also result in positive consequences. The accident can "reveal something absolutely necessary to knowledge." [11] For Virilio, the accident requires further analysis than the classic opposition between function and malfunction. The accident is even described as *hyperfunctional*. The accident shows a system in a state of entropy, and aids in the understanding of the system's normal functionality. This opens a domain for research and practice to which the arts singularly respond.

Glitches can exhibit a medium in a critical state, one that's unrecognizable and seemingly accidental. Catching a glimpse of this critical state can transform how a user perceives the medium's normal operation. Glitch aesthetics critique the medium itself, as a genre, interface, and expectation. They radically challenge the technological, habitual, or ideological construct of media formations by creating a point of critical reflection.

Notes

[1] Menkman, *The Glitch Moment(um)*, 9.
[2] Ibid., 26.
[3] Ernst Hans Josef Gombrich, *The Sense of Order: A Study in the Psychology of Decorative Art* (London: Phaidon Press, 1984), 9
[4] Menkman, *The Glitch Moment(um)*, 29.
[5] Ibid. Flow is emphasized by Menkman as both a trait within the machine as well as a feature of society as a whole. Menkman draws on Deleuze and Guitarri, who describe flow in terms of the beliefs and desires that both stimulate and maintain society. Flow comes into existence over long periods of time, during which conventions are established. In this case, deviations become rarefied and often understood as accidents, or glitches.
[6] Menkman, *The Glitch Moment(um)*, 30.
[7] Eric Kluitenberg, *Delusive Spaces: Essays on Culture, Media and Technology* (Rotterdam: NAi Publishers and Amsterdam: Institute of Network Cultures (2008), 357.
[8] Eric Kluitenberg, "Transfiguration of the Avant-Garde/The Negative Dialectics of the Net" (2002), accessed June 24, 2014, http://www.nettime.org/Lists-Archives/nettime-l-0201/msg00104.html.
[9] Menkman, *The Glitch Moment(um)*, 31.
[10] Paul Virilio and Julie Rose, *The Original Accident* (Cambridge: Polity Press) 2007, 10.
[11] Ibid.

5.0
Toward a Definition of Net Art

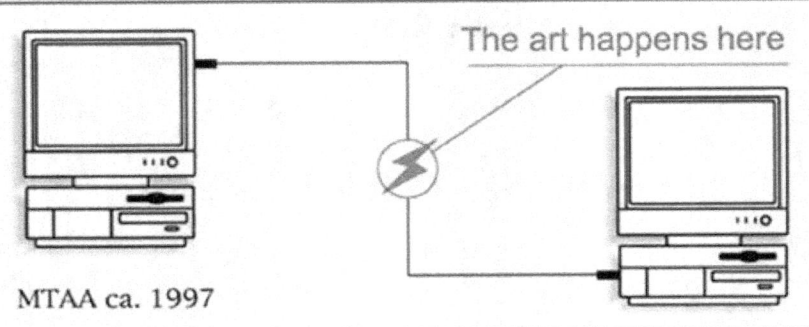

Fig. 6 MTAA, *Simple Net Art Diagram*, 1997. Gif animation.
www.mtaa.net/mtaaRR/off-line_art/snad.html

"In the process of defining and analyzing the differential specificity of this medium, we end up inside its various sub technologies and the more fleeting nature of the material: such as computer technologies, the basic Internet protocols plus the Net's incorporation and adaptation of personal media (diaries and photo albums) , magazines, newspapers, radio, television and telephones, and, last but not least, its social and cultural phenomena." — *Josephine Bosma*, Nettitudes: Let's Talk Net Art

The fact that a clear definition of Internet art has yet to be established signals the lack of institutional approval of the Internet as an appropriate medium for art practice. Texts on the subject of Internet art often list a broad range of tactics rather than approach a common conceptual, or technical, denominator. [1] German historian Tilman Baumgärtel defines net art in his first book as "art that deals with the genuine characteristics of the Internet and that can only happen through and with the Internet." [2] This position is revised in his later publication: "Net art, as I see the term, reaches above and beyond artistic projects that focus on the Internet." [3] New media critic Josephine Bosma has theorized about the domain of net art since the early 1990s. In her book *Nettitudes: Let's Talk Net Art*, she defines Internet art, in its most simple terms, as art based either on or within Internet cultures. In Bosma's definition, "culture" is intended in its broadest sense, including its intrinsic connection to technology as described by French philosopher Gilbert Simondon. [4] Net art results from a keen awareness of our intensely Internet-mediated lives, so it requires a definition that is as broad as the Internet itself.

If Duchamp redefined art through the act of selection, we have all become descendants of his aesthetic revolution insofar as our hyperconnected culture is predicated upon selection and remixing. [5] Internet art may appear to be little more than a whimsical endeavor characterized by a derivative aesthetic of popular media and network branding; but it constitutes nothing short of an anti-environment in an era of imperceptibility. By this, I mean that it offers the user a perspectival awareness of an interface-mediated environment that would otherwise remain unnoticed.

From a historical perspective, it might be tempting to view the determining role that the Internet has taken within visual arts communities simply as an extension of the dissemination of the arts in pre-existing mediums (i.e. print media, film, radio, TV, etc.); however, the Internet seems to represent something absolutely new in terms of flexibility, immediacy, and autonomous production. The Internet has demonstrated significant community-building potential since its inception. It can support, expand, and even create its own publics through publication just as print media and other forms of linear communication have in the past. [6] However, Internet media come into being a priori as dissemination and reproduction and thus, quite unlike print media, incite a nonlinear distribution of thought.

The net.art community of the 1990s seized the distributive potential of the Internet much like Fluxus artists seized the distributive potential of print media and the postal delivery system in the form of artist books and mail art. In their 1999 manifesto, "Introduction to Net.Art 1994-1999" Natalie Bookchin and Alexei Shulgin call upon their fellow artists to critique and subvert various modes of institutional control:

1. Definition
a. net.art is a self-defining term created by a malfunctioning piece of software, originally used to describe an art and communications activity on the internet.
b. net.artists sought to break down autonomous disciplines and outmoded classifications imposed upon various activists practices [sic.].
2. 0% Compromise
a. By maintaining independence from institutional bureaucracies
b. By working without marginalization and achieving substantial audience, communication, dialogue and fun
c. By realizing ways out of entrenched values arising from structured system of theories and ideologies
d. T.A.Z. (temporary autonomous zone) of the late 90s: Anarchy and spontaneity
3. Realization over Theorization
a. The utopian aim of closing the ever widening gap between art and everyday life, perhaps, for the first time, was achieved and became a real, everyday and even routine practice.
b. Beyond institutional critique: whereby an artist/individual could be equal to and on the same level as any institution or corporation.
c. The practical death of the author [7]

These statements articulate a particular attitude behind net.art created in the mid- and late 1990s, that is to say, during the era of Web 1.0. These works constituted a subversively imaginative, non-institutional, activist countermovement. The radically "relational" practice of net.art was detached from both the gallery space and the art commodity. Youthful, escapist, or utopian enthusiasms still transpire in network-based art, albeit often across various environments. Post-Internet stresses a confluence of issues and media involved in the shift from making art exclusively online, to making art that directly references the Internet as a cultural environment. In a sense, the term itself reflects the evolution of the practice that occurred between Web 1.0 and Web 2.0; it transpires from a reluctance toward medium-specific terms like browser-based art and net art. It is evident, now more than ever, that Internet art actually reaches beyond the confines of the World Wide Web and that a shared mechanism or tool does not alone constitute a shared aesthetic practice.

In many ways, a critical study of Internet art must be predicated upon an analysis of the avant-garde–it's indebted to avant-garde art practices inasmuch as it emphasizes the transfer of information, the use of networks, and the engagement of its audience. "The system of digital mediation, and in particular the sphere of networked digital communication, presents itself as a highly productive domain for critical strategies and artistic intervention," writes Kluitenberg. "Interestingly, it is the legacy of the avant-gardes of the last century that provides an enormously useful set of conceptual tools and references to develop a critical engagement with the conditions of digital mediation." [8] Much like avant-garde artists, Internet artists forgo the autonomous status, or aura, traditionally ascribed to art objects. The practices that have influenced net art share a common interest in shifting art away from traditional representation. Not unlike the Dada and Fluxus artworks of the early twentieth century, much net art is employed as a critique, or subversion, of the assumptions built into new or existing structures.

Dadaists drew upon arbitrary patterns, chance operations, and rhythmical noise to produce various forms of "self-generative" works In doing so, they rejected conventions of perfection and order, which they viewed as bourgeois values. In the Dada manifesto of 1918, Tristan Tzara makes the claim: "I am against systems, the most acceptable system is on principle to have none." [9] Tzara famously advised aspiring poets to cut newspaper articles into single words and generate poetry by shaking them out of a bag at random, at once revealing hidden possibilities of language and undermining notions of creative genius or authority. This act both predates and guides the anti-authorial tone of Shulgin's heed. As Tzara explains, "These phonetic poems... totally renounce the language that journalism has abused and corrupted." [10] The rejection of a habituated system of language calls its implicit universality and directness into question. The automatic texts of the Dadaists demeaned the significance of the poet, turning the text into a transcription, or discovery, rather than a production, or invention. The Internet finds an analog to this text in programming language, as this forms the basis of all computer operations. Through the manipulation of code, Internet artists question the implicit conditions of the network and interface, just as Dadaists questioned the implicit conditions of language itself.

Notes

[1] Bosma, *Nettitudes*, 29. This tendency is also present in the major exhibitions of net art thus far: *Documenta X* in 1997, and *Net Condition* at the Zentrum für Kunst und Medien (ZKM) in Karlsruhe in 1999.

[2] Tilman Baumgärtel, *[net.art]*, trans. Josephine Bosma in *Nettitudes: Let's Talk Net Art* (Rotterdam: NAi Publishers, 2011), 30.

[3] Ibid.

[4] Bosma, *Nettitudes*, 29. See also Gilbert Simondon, *On the Mode of Existence as a Technological Object* (Paris: Aubier, 2001). According to Simondon, technology and culture cannot be separated. The technological environment has a strong, intrinsic potential to become a thriving, cultural space.

[5] David Crawford, *Art and the Real-Time Archive*, 40.

[6] I, of course, use the word publication loosely in order to denote the Internet's extension from Gutenberg technologies as a form of making information public, and formalizing it in some capacity in the act of public posting, as well as making it available for adaptation and reinterpretation.

[7] Natalie Bookchin and Alexei Shulgin, "Introduction to Net.art," *subsol index*, 1999, accessed May 1, 2014, http://subsol.c3.hu/subsol_2/contributors/bookchin-text.html.

[8] Kluitenberg, "Transfiguration of the Avant-Garde."

[9] Tristan Tzara, "Dada Manifesto," in Charles Harrison and Paul Wood, *Art in Theory: 1900-1990: An Anthology of Changing Ideas* (Oxford: Blackwell, 1998), 249—253.

[10] Tristan Tzara, "Dada Manifesto," 249—253.

6.0
Making the
Invisible
Visible

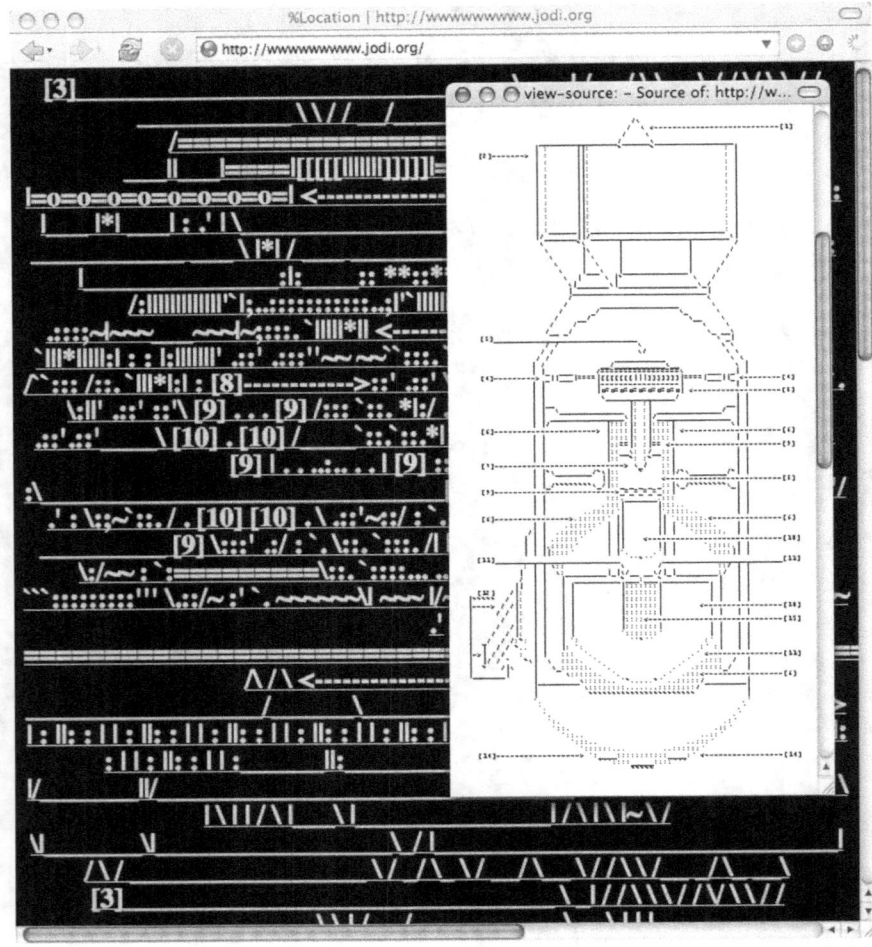

Fig. 7 Jodi.org, http://wwwwww.jodi.org/, 1995. Screenshot.

"Contemporariness is, then, a singular relationship with one's own time, which adheres to it and, at the same time, keeps a distance from it. More precisely, it is that relationship with time that adheres to it through a disjunction and an anachronism." — *Giorgio Agamben,* What Is the Contemporary?

Jodi.org is both a website and a moniker for its creators, Joan Heemskerk and Dirk Paesmans, a Dutch-Belgian artist couple. [1] The site represents one of the earliest forays into code abstraction. Heemskerk and Paesmans were part of a network of artists who rejected digital art in the form of "interactive," high-tech graphic simulations in favor of ironic, low-tech forms that played with anachronism and software disruption. They created aggressively obvious interfaces, abandoning coherent content in favor of glitches and code disclosures. [2] Contrary to slick, visually immersive digital art, Jodi exposes the computational process as an absurd conflation of contingent data streams, and does so through an aesthetic of malfunction.

At *http://wwwwww.jodi.org/* [*fig. 7*], website visitors are confronted with a black webpage, decorated with an array of neon green text symbols. The tabular numbers, colons and dashes convey a sense of cryptic error messages. The webpage is repetitive discordant, and alphanumeric, but the images are not what they appear to be: behind the image lies a source code. This visualization of code language appears as a cascade of diagrammatic ASCII patterns. [3] The piece seems to divide and radicalize the interface, confounding preconceptions of its inherent "lightness" or seamlessness; indeed, *http://wwwwww.jodi.org/* is the product of a relentless search for bugs and deviations that many net artists consider essential to understanding the medium. Design flaws, or perhaps even "design surpluses," wind up revealing the true nature of the interface. The

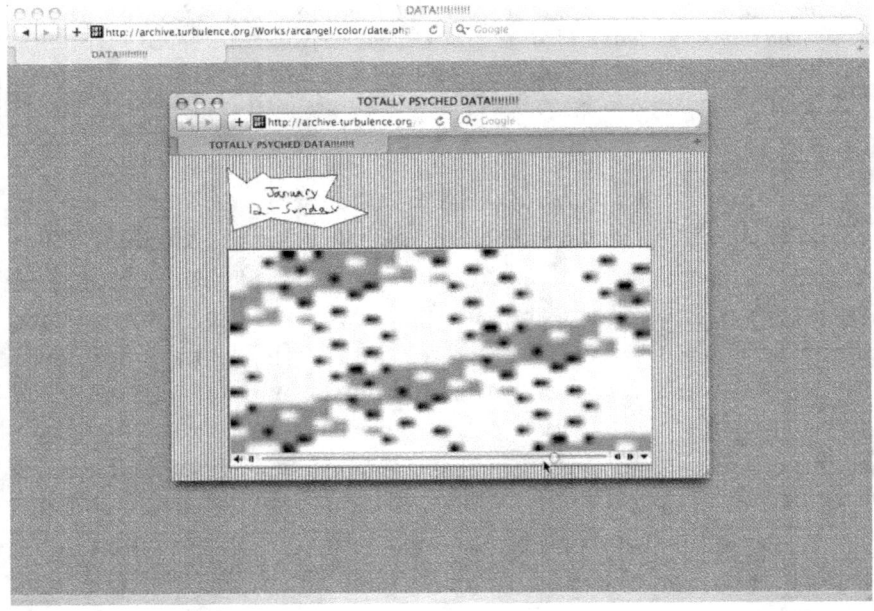

:(){ :|:& };:

Fig. 8 Cory Arcangel, *Data Diaries*, 2002. Screenshot. http://archive.turbulence.org/Works/arcangel/
Fig. 9 Denis Jaromil Rojo, *Forkbomb*, 2012. Screenshot. http://www.transmediale.de/content/forkbomb-shell

artists' conflation of code fragments, character encodings, markup languages and network protocol code combine to become a navigable webpage composed of collage and concrete poetry.

Many early Internet artists continued, in this vein, to initiate projects that demystify, domesticate, and familiarize the interface. In Cory Arcangel's *Data Diaries* [*fig. 8*], for instance, the artist infringes upon the formatted structure of the hard drive by feeding its random-access memory archive (RAM) into a QuickTime player application. [4] In essence, the piece translates the medium of computer data into the visual, time-based medium of a video file. The resulting data conversion produces a brilliant array of blocks of primary color, flickering across the screen as though the computer is defragmenting itself. [5] Arcangel subverts the assumption of smooth, operational processes and produces radical anti-design; the finished product is the result of an application reading a file that it is not programmed to read. The Italian programmer and artist Denis Jaromil Rojo, known as Jaromil, created a similarly challenging piece for the first exhibition of computer viruses as artworks at the Museum of Applied Arts in Frankfurt. [6] Jaromil is a leading figure in both European media-art and free-software activist circles. His work *Forkbomb* [*fig. 9*] consists of a minimal string of symbols that endlessly replicate themselves when typed into a command line, resulting in the computer's mechanical failure. This particular type of "virus" is known as a forkbomb because its execution operates through a "fork reaction." Jaromil's work successfully unites ideas of networking, artistic experimentation, hacking, and political activism. [7] "The digital domain produces a form of chaos," Jaromil writes; "to surf thru [sic] in that chaos viruses are spontaneous compositions, lyrical in causing imperfections in machines made to

Fig. 10 The Jogging, *VARIOUS PERSONAL BRANDS ASSOCIATED WITH THE JOGGING, COMBINED*, 2012. Screenshot. http://thejogging.tumblr.com/post/24687665454/various-personal-brands-associated-with-the

serve." [8] *Forkbomb* could be understood as a marriage between Jaromil's work as an artist and as a coder. More importantly, though, it reveals a sensitive lyricism in the unfolding of its image, which begins after someone types the simple code into the command line of a basic, Unix-based computer system. [9]

As Bosma suggests, it is no longer necessary for Internet art to use the Internet as its primary medium — as it can use networked culture in and of itself. In this sense, network-based art obviously diverges from other mediums of art making for which the Internet does not play a principal role. The careful curation of digital images, coding, and documentation responds to radical changes in image-making and distribution.

Former curatorial models that rely on physical space and the exchange of physical objects, like paintings and sculptures, are increasingly undermined by distributed viewership online. In order to address the process of subjectification engendered by the vanishing interface, it could be the case that net art actively *exposes* the temporal and spatial modes of the virtual. It offers articulations through the ubiquitous web, albeit with the distinct perspective that a gallery experience might offer — engagement and removal, reflection and transference.

There are a multitude of projects that suit this trajectory, however, for the sake of brevity, they won't all be listed here in grave detail. Instead, I will outline a few exemplary cases beginning with *The Jogging* [*fig. 10*], a collaborative experiment led by artists Brad Troemel and Lauren Christiansen. *The Jogging* utilizes Tumblr, a micro-blogging platform, as a space for displaying digitally manipulated art objects. Their site famously functions as a stream of image concepts executed with immediacy and inherent repeatability, exempt from physical or institutional limitations. [10] *The Jogging* is an art object comprised of many image files, each submitted by an anonymous user. Anonymity and multitude contribute to *The Jogging*'s curious ability to function both as a conceptual artwork and abstract machine. Many of the digital images contributed to *The Jogging* are extracted from Google image searches and re-composited in editing software like Adobe Photoshop. Each piece functions as the documentation of an object, installation, or performance that never existed and perhaps never could. [11] As a statement issued on the site in 2010, states:

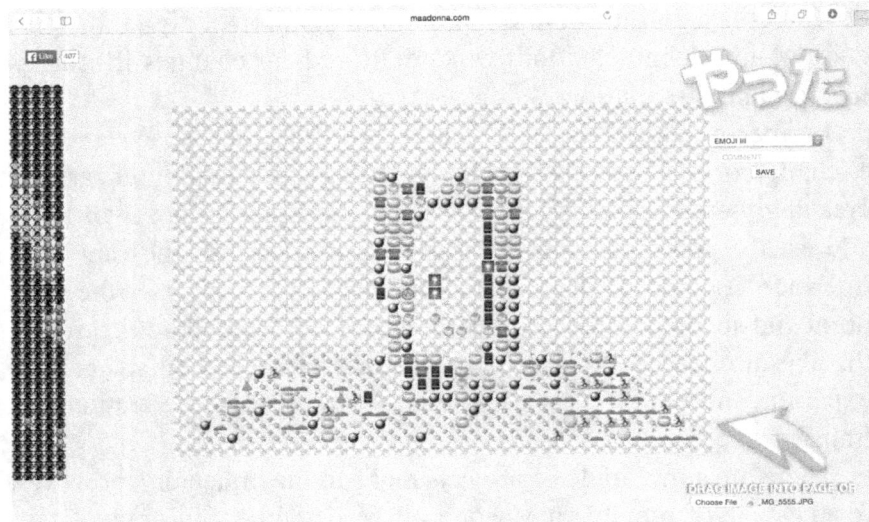

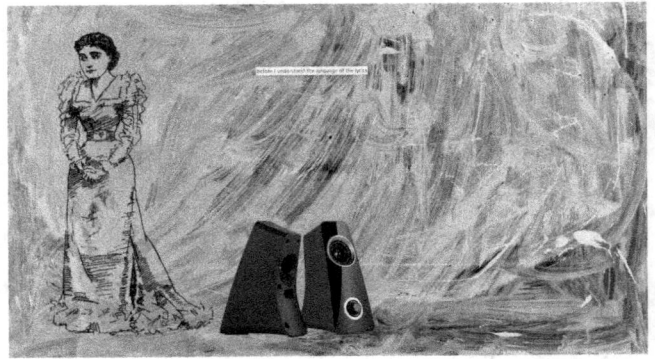

Fig. 11 Emilio Gomariz and Kim Asendorf, *Maadonna*, 2012. Screenshot. http://maadonna.com
Fig. 12 Harm Van Dorpel, *Deep Tissue*, 2014. Screenshot. http://deeptis.su/e

By multiplying the potential for consumerist relationships the inter-net [sic] offers great chances for efficiency in viewership. However, the internet [sic] also introduces new social conditions that do not fit within characteristically modern organizations. This is to say that if we understand the internet [sic] solely as a device to retrieve art still at home in the modernist institution, we are still relying on an out-dated, vertical model of information acquisition. We should instead encourage horizontally organized methods that decentralize informa-tion, as these are the models [that] actively engage the radical new potential for information's transmission. [12]

Aligning with the sentiment of Fluxus projects or Happenings, net art problematizes the role of the artist by removing his physi-cal index from the production, dissemination, and reception of the artwork. Not only does Internet art vary according to external data conditions or user input, it varies by virtue of its constantly shifting medium (i.e. upgraded software and applications, abandoned web pages).

This is, in part, why utilizing the symbols and abstractions of networked connectivity, or creating associations that implicate one's audience, are such resonant features of much network-based art. Works like *Maadonna* [*fig. 11*] by Emilio Gomariz and Kim Asendorf, and *Deep Tissue* [*fig. 12*] by Harm Van Dorpel, tend to appropriate the very language of software branding, meanwhile en-couraging new navigational patterns and viewing behaviors. Many works created within the last decade exist in this manner: as static or responsive landing pages that directly manipulate familiar ap-plications, programs, and commands. But a wide range of Internet artists have also extended their practices beyond the screen, con-structing temporary, physically variable architectures that carefully re-examine the actions inherent to interface mediation.

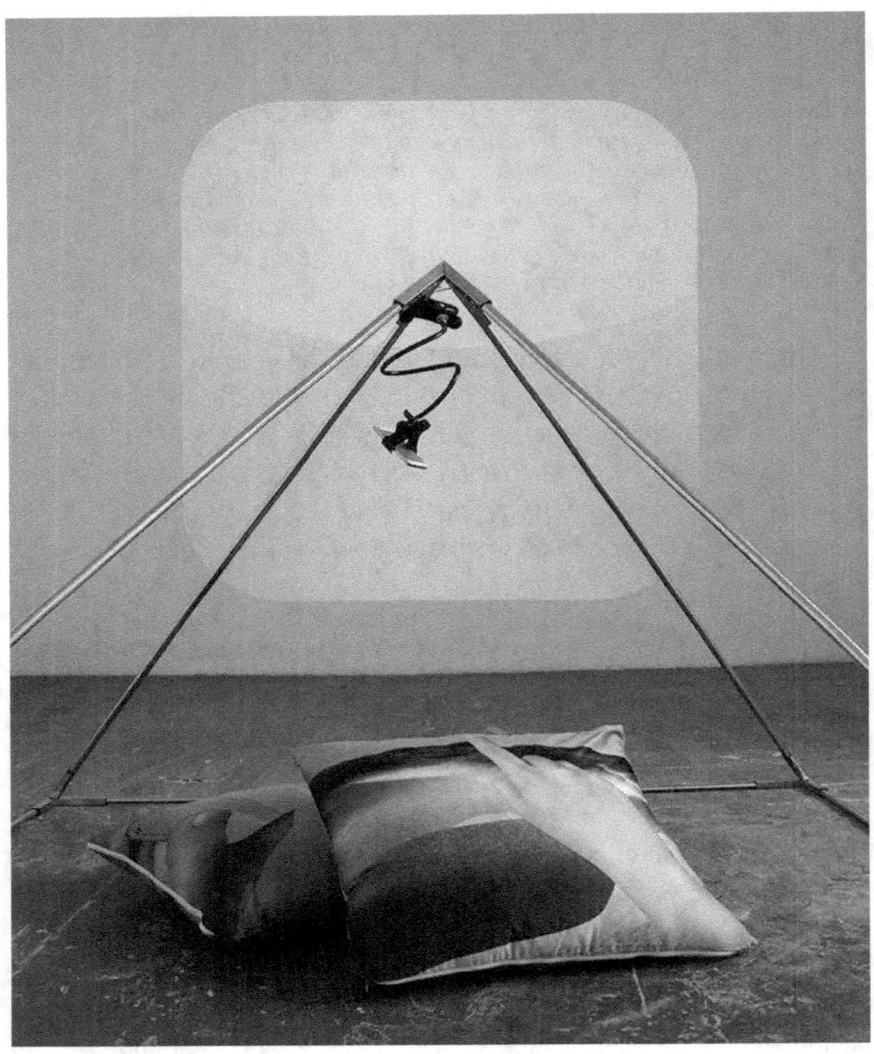

Fig. 13 Miao Ying, *APP-Nosis*, 2013-14. Installation view, courtesy the artist.

Miao Ying's *APP-nosis* [*fig. 13*] deconstructs the meaning of the mobile application by providing an acutely aware atmosphere for viewers to experience the app in. The piece includes three metal structures, or, "Meditation Pyramids." [13] Each pyramid presents the viewer with a gold-edition iPhone 5S to gaze into while laying on real beds of grass, surrounded by pillows. The pillows are emblazoned with chromakeyed compositions, each uniting the hands of touchscreen advertisements with artificial landscapes. [14]

The application itself shows the movement of shifting color, accompanied by a soundtrack of stereotypically relaxing music. [15] *APP-nosis* seems to act as an antithesis to the typical mobile application: it is not in the least user-friendly, and it does little to disguise its margins or parts. Contrarily, it is highly stylized and highly obtrusive, making its own artificiality pretty conspicuous. *APP-nosis* even removes the only legible part of the app icon — its logo.

Dutch artist Anne de Vries' practice similarly breaks with user preconceptions of functionality. His interests in ergonomic material and human flows, or more precisely, how these translate into data flows, are manifest in his art. de Vries modulates the conditions of objects like handrails, commercial beams, and screens, in order to produce novel tendencies [*see fig. 14*]. [16] By dismantling common notions of what these technologies are, and what they do, de Vries provides suppositional instances of *what they could be*. This deconstructive gesture muses on forms of detachment and attention-deficit that the seamless interface has brought to new heights.

Recall that much Internet art seems to eschew high-resolution images in favor of substandard resolution ones: thumbnails, .JPEGs, .GIFS, and moving-image files that are then compressed,

Fig. 14 Anne de Vries, *Air Gap Hold On*, 2013. Digital print on towel, stainless steel, pla-stic.107 x 65 x 8 cm, courtesy the artist

ripped, and reproduced across various networks of distribution. Many of these works inevitably hearken the design aesthetic of Web 1.0, and continue the proliferation of visuals sourced from out-dated web cameras, mobile phones, home computers, and other forms of image capture. These images insist upon their own error and imperfection. But in doing so, they also draw attention to the multiple connections and erratic links behind interface mediation.

Network-based artists intuit a visual understanding of computational activity and networked participation. Autodidacts and amateurs are seldom considered a positive force; however, within networked art and cultures, they are at the very center of a movement that reclaims a sense of agency. The pervasive, indeterminate network of interfaces may create a set of conditions for the avant-garde to resurface; for amateurs, so to speak, to act increasingly as producers of reality.

Notes

[1] Greene, *Internet Art*, 40.

[2] Ibid.

[3] ASCII is the American Standard Code for Information Interchange, with the four foundational font characters of 8-bit Block ASCII. These shapes were originally found in the 1979 character set Code Page 437, or CP437, of the original IBM PC.

[4] Greene, *Internet Art*, 200.

[5] Defragmenting is a computing process that reduces the fragmentation of files by linking parts stored in separate locations on a disk.

[6] Bosma, *Nettitudes*, 73.

[7] Tatiana Bazzichelli, *Networking: The Net as Artwork* (Aarhus, Denmark: Aarhus University Press, 2008), 189.

[8] Bosma, *Nettitudes*, 73—74

[9] Ibid.

[10] The "reblog" function of the site allows users to share media with ease. While it attempts to maintain a chain of attribution, images are frequently stripped and reposted to begin new chains with new "authors," such that image producers knowingly lose control of their work upon posting it to the site.

[11] Jacob Gaboury, "Immaterial Incoherence: Art Collective Jogging," *Rhizome*, May 5, 2010, accessed May 16, 2014, http://rhizome.org/editorial/2010/may/5/immaterial-incoherence/.

[12] "Redefining Exhibition in the Digital Age," *The Jogging Archive 2009—2010*, March 29, 2010, accessed May 16, 2014, http://thejoggingarchive.tumblr.com/post/11304614393/redefining-exhibition-in-the-digital-age.

[13] Iona Whittaker, "Miao Ying.gif Island," *ArtReview*, January/February 2015, 152.

[14] Whittaker, "Miao Ying.gif Island," *ArtReview*, January/February 2015,152.

[15] Ibid.

[16] See Anne de Vries, "Recent Work by Anne de Vries," February 2015, 41. accessed March 16, 2015, http://annedevries.info/cat/pdf/portfolio/.

Conclusion

"The poor image is no longer about the real thing — the originary original. Instead, it is about its own real conditions of existence: about swarm circulation, digital dispersion, fractured and flexible temporalities. It is about defiance and appropriation just as it is about conformism and exploitation. In short: it is about reality." — Hito Steyerl, "In Defense of the Poor Image"

Interface design assumes technology can, or should, seem immaterial. While the goal of designing a purely transparent interface is unobtainable, innovation nevertheless seems to require that an interface interfere with the user experience as little as possible. This design principle encourages the user to forget about the presence of the medium and to believe in the directness of immediate transmission. In the words of media critics Jay David Bolter and Richard Grusin, "[O]ur culture wants to multiply its media and to erase all traces of mediation: ideally, it wants to erase its media in the very act of multiplying them." It is the very "logic of immediacy," according to Bolter and Grusin, which "dictates that the medium itself should disappear." [1]

The extent to which the interface suffuses everyday life is attested by the development of what is increasingly referred to as the "Internet of Things." This phrase describes the communication between the Internet and uniquely identifiable objects, effectively enabling the Internet to reach into dimensions of physical space. [2] The term "real-time" describes the instantaneity of information technology. Real-time computing requires the operating system to respond to commands without perceivable delay. These two forms of computing development illustrate how the complexity and speed of new technology can cause both euphoria and anxiety. [3] The increasing demand for instant feedback and response provides a new sense of urgency that segments our attention and imposes low-level, reactive panic. In a hyperconnected society, the operation of an interface is a highly orchestrated event — requiring the user to dedicate a significant amount of perceptual and mental resources to the very act.

The interface presents us with a flattened landscape of digital information. [4] Massive quantities of data generated by network communications are regulated in terms we can't easily comprehend. [5] According to Flusser, information technology marks the return of the age-old concept of "matter" as a temporary filling of eternal forms. [6] Although we might be able to effortlessly click, drag, and delete media, it remains that code and computation are backed by a set of programmatic rules that lie beyond our control. [7]

Network-based art practices can function as an aesthetic critique of our relationship with digital media. As Belgian RFID analyst Rob van Kranenberg notes, "We are entering a land where the environment has become the interface." [8] The interface, however, is not necessarily impenetrable, solid, or static. It can be breached, and intervention of the interface is critical to our continued perception of the physical, material world. One critical difference between Internet art and "other" art is that the work generally will not disclose itself without specific modes of engagement with interface technology. Internet art constructs variable modes of anachronism and anti-design, reconstituting the user's expectation for otherwise transparent interface mediation. Planned obsolescence and nostalgia have made the gap between new and old technologies both smaller and more dialectical. [9] Although obsolescence and retromediation used to be closely connected to the factor of linear time, this factor has become more fractal, resulting in a transformation of the anachronistic, or avant-garde, tendencies of Internet Art.

It could be argued that, in light of both hyper-connectivity and real-time computing, obsolescence is always immanent. This can be observed in the rapid migration and subsequent demise of those image objects on the web known as "memes." In her study, "In Defense of the Poor Image", Hito Steyerl suggests that both the quality of "copy in motion," and substandard resolution, of outmoded image files–compressed, reproduced and pasted into various channels of distribution–actively encourage the participation of a much larger group of producers. [10] These images reveal the collective editing, file sharing circuits, and erratic links between the producers and programs that make them possible. In short, their path from sudden dispersion to complete obsolescence allow us to see the apparatus in terms of its very real conditions. Many network-based art projects are precisely about reality: the artist constructs a deliberately outmoded space, be it online or offline, wherein the navigation and perception central to the interface is subtly controlled and manipulated. They mock the entire promise of digital technology. By confounding the narrow conception of the interface and its functions, Internet art offers the potential to recognize the machine as an apparatus. [11]

As American curator Steve Dietz has stated, "art is different after New Media because of new media — not because New Media is 'next,' but because its behaviors are the behaviors of our technological times." [12] Agamben's articulation of the contemporary, as one who firmly holds his gaze on his own time, predates Dietz's observation. [13] For Agamben, perceiving the obscurity of one's own time is not a form of passivity, but instead a singular and active ability. Contemporariness can be found in a relationship that adheres to time through disjunction. The avant-garde must pursue the primitive and the archaic. [14] The radical momentum and conceptuality of net.art was, initially, a way for artists to critique the social and economical drive behind the development of new technologies. To call net art a genre is to suggest that it is intelligible as a tendency — a tendency to exploit medium-reflexivity and to interrogate the perfect use and function of technological convention and expectation. [15] As a form of anachronism and anti-design, network-based art can aid the understanding of interface mediation, making the invisible visible and undeniable, subverting media constructions and providing the perceptual conditions for subjective autonomy.

Notes

[1] Jay David Bolter and Richard Grusin, *Remediation: Understanding New Media* (Cambridge, MA: MIT Press,1999), 5—6.

[2] Rob van Kranenberg, *The Internet of Things: A Critique of Ambient Technology and the All-Seeing Network of RFID*, accessed April 7, 2014, http://www.networkcultures.org/_uploads/notebook2_theinternetofthings.pdf.

[3] Charlie Gere, *Art, Time, and Technology* (New York: Bloomsbury Academic, 2006), 1.

[4] In *Networked: A (networked_book) about (networked_art)*, Anna Munster notes that even when data flows "freely" through the net, the operations of search engines, databases, digests and feeds such as RSS increasingly makes this manipulation of data invisible. Data aggregation refers to the process of redefining data into a summarization based on a set of criteria. accessed December 12, 2013, http://munster.networkedbook.org.

[5] Munster, *Networked*.

[6] Flusser, *The Shape of Things*, 23.

[7] Florian Cramer, *Words Made Flesh: Code, Culture, Imagination*, 8.

[8] van Kranenberg, *The Internet of Things*.

[9] Menkman, *The Glitch Moment(um)*, 57.

[10] Hito Steyerl, "In Defense of the Poor Image," *e-flux 10* (2009): 1, accessed July 22, 2015, http://www.e-flux.com/journal/in-defense-of-the-poor-image/.

[11] Again, I use "apparatus" in Agamben's sense of the term, e.g., an object that can determine, or secure, the gestures and behaviors of living beings. For further discussion, see Agamben, *What is an Apparatus*, 14.

[12] Bosma, *Nettitudes*, 60.

[13] Agamben, *What Is an Apparatus?*, 44.

[14] Ibid.

[15] Menkman, *The Glitch Moment(um)*, 56.

Bibliography

Aarseth, Espen J. *Cybertext: Perspectives On Ergodic Literature*. Baltimore: Johns Hopkins University Press, 1997.

Agamben, Giorgio. *What Is an Apparatus? And Other Essays*. Stanford, CA: Stanford University Press, 2009.

Antonellis, Anthony. *Impulse 101: An Essay About Art, the Internet, and Everything*. Master's Thesis, Bauhaus-Universität Weimar, 2011.

Baudrillard, Jean. "The Ecstasy of Communication." In *The Anti-Aesthetic: Essays On Postmodern Culture*. Edited by Hal Foster, 125—133 Seattle: Bay Press, 1995.

Bazzichelli, Tatiana. *Networking: The Net as Artwork*. Aarhus, Denmark: Aarhus University Press, 2008.

Benjamin, Walter. "A Small History of Photography." In Walter Benjamin: *One Way Street and Other Writings*. Translated by Edmund Jephcott and Kingsley Shorter, 240—257 London: Verso, 1985.

Bolter, Jay David, and Richard Grusin. *Remediation: Understanding New Media*. Cambridge, MA: The MIT Press, 1999.

Bookchin, Natalie, and Alexei Shulgin. "Introduction to Net.art." *subsol index*. 1999. Accessed May 1, 2014. http://subsol.c3.hu/subsol_2/contributors/bookchintext.html.

Bosma, Josephine. *Nettitudes: Let's Talk Net Art*. Rotterdam: NAi Publishers, 2011.

Couchot, Edmond. "The Automatization of Figurative Techniques: Towards the Autonomous Image." In *MediaArtHistories*, Edited by Oliver Grau, 181—92. Cambridge, MA: MIT Press, 2007.

Cramer, Florian. "Digital Code and Literary Text." *netzliteratur. net*. Accessed May 13, 2014. http://www.netzliteratur.net/cramer/digital_code_and_literary_text.html.

Cramer, Florian. *Words Made Flesh: Code, Culture, Imagination*. netzliteratur.net. Accessed April 7, 2014, http://www.netzliteratur.net/cramer/wordsmadefleshpdf.pdf.

Crawford, David. "Art and the Real-Time Archive: Remix, Relocation, Response." *turbulence.org*. Accessed December 11, 2013. http://www.turbulence.org/studios/crawford/art_and_the_real_time_archive.pdf.

Ferguson, Bruce W., Reesa Greenberg, and Sandy Nairne, Editors. *Thinking about Exhibitions*. London: Routledge, 1996.

Flusser, Vilém. *The Shape of Things*. London: Reaktion Books, 1999.

Gere, Charlie. *Art, Time, and Technology*. New York: Bloomsbury Academic, 2006.

Greene, Rachel. *Internet Art*. New York: Thames & Hudson, 2004.

Gombrich, Ernst. *The Sense of Order: A Study in the Psychology of Decorative Art*. London, England: Phaidon Press, 1979.

Gumbrecht, Hans Ulrich. "A Farewell to Interpretation." In *Materialities of Communication*, Edited by Hans Ulrich Gumbrecht and K. Ludwig Pfeiffer, 389—402. Stanford: Stanford University Press, 1994.

Hayles, N. Katherine. *Electronic Culture: Technology and Visual Representation*. New York: Aperture Foundation, 1996.

de Kerckhove, Derrick. *The Skin of Culture: Investigating the New Electronic Reality*. Edited by Christopher Dewdney. Toronto: Somerville House Books, 1995.

Kluitenberg, Eric. *Delusive Spaces. Essays on Culture, Media and Technology*. Rotterdam: NAi Publishers and Amsterdam: Institute of Network Cultures, 2008.

van Kranenberg, Rob. "The Internet of Things. A Critique of Ambient Technology and the All-seeing Network of RFID." *networkcultures.org*, Accessed April 7, 2014. http://www.networkcultures.org/_uploads/notebook2_theinternetofthings.pdf.

Krauss, Rosalind. *A Voyage on the North Sea: Art in the Age of the Post-Medium Condition*. New York: Thames & Hudson, 2000.

Lacan, Jacques. *The Seminar of Jacques Lacan: The Ethics of Psychoanalysis (1959–1960)*. London: Routledge, 1992.

Mackenzie, Adrian. *Transductions: Bodies and Machines at Speed*. New York: Bloomsbury Academic, 2006.

Manovich, Lev. "Information as an Aesthetic Event." Lecture, Tate Modern, London, England, 2007. Accessed December 10, 2013, http://manovich.net/DOCS/TATE_lecture.doc.

Manovich, Lev. *The Language of New Media* (Leonardo Books). Cambridge, MA: The MIT Press, 2002.

Manovich, Lev. "The Practice of Everyday (Media) Life: From Mass Consumption to Mass Cultural Production." *Critical Inquiry* 35, no. 2 (Winter 2009): 319. Accessed December 3, 2013. http://www.jstor.org/stable/10.1086/596645.

McGugh, Gene. *Post Internet*. Brescia: LINK Editions, 2011.

McLuhan, Marshall. *Understanding Media: the Extensions of Man*. Cambridge, MA: The MIT Press, 1994.

McLuhan, Marshall, and Harley Parker. *Through the Vanishing Point: Space in Poetry and Painting*. New York: Harper & Row, 1968.

McLuhan, Marshall, and Quentin Fiore. *War and Peace in the Global Village*. Berkeley: Gingko Press, 2001.

Menkman, Rosa. *The Glitch Moment(um)*. Amsterdam: Institute of Network Cultures, 2011.

Munster, Anna. *Networked: a (networked book) about (networked art)*, Accessed December 12, 2013, http://munster.networkedbook.org/.

Postman, Neil. *Technopoly: The Surrender of Culture to Technology*. New York: Vintage, 1993.

Shulgin, Alexei. "Art, Power and Communication." *Nettime*. October 7, 1996. Accessed May 16, 2014. http://amsterdam.nettime.org/Lists-Archives/nettime-l-9610/msg00036.html.

Siegel, Lee. *Net of Magic: Wonders and Deceptions in India.* Chicago: University of Chicago Press, 1991.

Simondon, Gilbert. *On the Mode of Existence as a Technological Object*. Paris: Aubier, 2001.

Steyerl, Hito. "In Defense of the Poor Image." *e-flux 10* (2009): 1. Accessed July 22, 2015. http://www.e-flux.com/journal/in-defense-of-the-poor-image/.

Tzara, Tristan. "Dada Manifesto." *In Art in Theory, 1900—1990: An Anthology of Changing Ideas*, Edited by Charles Harrison & Paul Wood, 249—253 Oxford: Blackwell 1998.

Virilio, Paul and Julia Rose. *The Original Accident*. Cambridge, MA: Polity, 2007.

Whittaker, Iona. "Miao Ying.gif Island." *ArtReview*, January/February 2015.

Žižek, Slavoj. *The Plague of Fantasies*. London: Verso, 1997.

Žižek, Slavoj. *The Sublime Object of Ideology*. London: Verso, 1997.